GOD IS IN CHARGE!

This edition published in 2013

Cover Design by Jose Luna

Photography by Lindsey Luna

Published by Disciples Of the Word Ministries, Inc. Printed in the USA by L. Brown & Sons Printing.

ISBN 978-1-304-01253-1

Scripture quotations used in this book are from the NKJV unless noted otherwise.

Note: I want to express my gratitude to Dr. Dean Davis for teaching me the fundamentals of this approach to the book of Daniel.

GOD

Is In Charge!

Study Guide
by

Jose Luna

CONTENTS

We dedicate this lesson to God's people, those who are like the Bereans, "always searching the Word."

Definition of Terms

Covenant	A mutual treaty made between two parties.
Suzerain	The commanding ruler.
Vassal	A subject under authority of a Suzerain.
Courtier	A vassal who serves in the royal court.
Preterist	Prophetic events are in the past.
Futurist	Prophetic events are in the future.
Spiritualist	Prophetic events are all symbolic, there's no lineal history
A-millenial	Belief that there's no millennium (a thousand years).
Pre-millenial	The rapture will happen before the millennium.
Post-millenial	The rapture will happen after the millennium.
Millenial	There will be a 1000 years of judgment in heaven.
Prophet	Someone who teaches and prophesies of God's ways.
Theme	The main teaching in a particular writing.
Hittite	Ancient people who lived in the 18th century B.C.
Exile	Cast out of home and country.
Adamic	In reference to the covenant with Adam.
Davidic	In reference to the covenant with David.
Abrahamic	In reference to the covenant with Abraham.

Introduction

Historical Background
In 606/605 Nebuchadnezzar besieged Jerusalem and took Daniel and the royal family captive. In 597/596 he took Jehoiachim, Ezequiel and 10,000 upper class citizens captive. In 587/586, Jerusalem fell and he took Zedekiah and most of the inhabitants of Jerusalem captive.

Theological Background
God made a covenant (plan of salvation) with Adam, Abraham, Israel and David (2 Sam. 7). The Covenant with Abraham, Israel and David was based on the very well known Hittite covenant, where a suzerain (king or ruler) initiated the agreement with the vassal (inferior co-ruler). The superior suzerain elaborated on the covenant and the vassal could accept it or reject it. This covenant would contain the following points:

1. **Pre-amble** (Identification of the Covenant maker).
2. **Background** (historical relationship between the Suzerain and the vassal.
3. **Stipulations** (what is expected from both parties).
4. **Covenant Witnesses** (those who legalized the Covenant).
5. **Public reading** (promulgation of the Covenant).
6. **Blessings/Curses Formula** (rewards for Covenant fidelity).

God as the Supreme Suzerain would also do certain things such as:

- ✓ Unconditional covenant promises.
- ✓ He would give a probationary period to determine man's loyalty to the Covenant.
- ✓ He would also establish an investigative judgment to determine the reward in terms of blessings or curses.
- ✓ He would ultimately give the Rewards (blessings/curses).

Three Basics Elements of God's Covenant

1. Land
2. Seed
3. Reward

Any covenant that God has ever made with any human has always involved these three main elements and we will look into some examples in the next lesson.

Three Important Things to Remember

a) It is God who initiates the agreement.
b) It is God who would protect mankind from mankind main's predator (Satan).
c) It is up to us (mankind) to accept God's plan of salvation (covenant) for us.

What Should We Expect From This Lesson

- ✓ To learn that God is in control of human history.
- ✓ To know that no matter how rooted evil seems to be, God has already predicted in details its destruction.
- ✓ To trust the covenant Maker (God).
- ✓ To be covenant keepers of God's perfect covenant for us.
- ✓ To establish a firm foundation on the importance of the Scriptures as the inspired word of God.
- ✓ To see the hand of God moving throughout history.
- ✓ To determine on which side we are (good or evil).

Let's begin our amazing journey by simply defining what a covenant is:

"***A covenant is a legal agreement made between two parties that establishes regulations, commitment, privileges, rewards and responsibilities for each person involved***" (Luna, 2000).

Three Main Covenants To Look At!

"And this is my covenant with them when I take away their sins." (Rom. 11; 27).

The Adamic Covenant

- ✓ Land (Eden).
- ✓ Seed (be fruitful and multiply).
- ✓ Blessings (man was a co-ruler with God over the earth).

God provided all the needs for Adam and Eve, based on His function as Suzerain (Protector). Even after the fall of man into sin, God appeared again unto him and made the same promises (Gen. 3; 15).

The Abrahamic Covenant

a) Land (Canaan)
b) Seed (Isaac, the son of the promise).
c) Blessing (father of many nations)

God appeared unto Abraham and initiated the covenant with him. This establishes the consistency of God's pattern: always reaching out to man as the Suzerain of the universe.

The Davidic Covenant

- ✓ Land (eternal Davidic kingdom - 2 Sam. 7; 16).
- ✓ Seed (eternal Davidic line of kings - 2 Sam. 7; 11-12).
- ✓ Blessing (David's kingdom would be forever - 2 Sam. 7; 14-16).

Once more, it is God who would initiate the covenant with his vassal king David (in this case). And in doing so, God was sending a very powerful message of consistency to all of us.

In each one of these cases, God intended to direct our attention towards the fulfillment of the covenant in the person of Jesus Christ as the Messiah, this means that:

a) The Messiah is the true Offspring of Adam, Abraham and David. It was never intended to be Seth, Isaac or Solomon.

b) The Messiah is the "Offspring" promised to Adam. The "Seed" promised to Abraham and the ultimate King or Ruler of the Davidic line of kings promised to David.
c) Ultimately, the Messiah's kingdom will be eternal.

Some Unique Considerations

- ✓ God will always fulfill His promises.
- ✓ God's promises are unconditional from His standpoint of view (He never changes).
- ✓ This means that if the "chosen ones reject the covenant" God still will find someone who can fulfill it.

What Happened Then?

We said in the introduction that Nebuchadnezzar entered Jerusalem and destroyed it with fire, and took captive 10,000 people from the royal tribe (Judah).

We ask ourselves the question. What happened? Did God break His part of the agreement? Or are there major underlying reasons why the whole covenant concept seemed to fall apart, especially after David's death?

Reasons For the Destruction of Jerusalem

1. The people became covenant-breakers on a daily basis.
2. The people established covenants with other gods.
3. The people were not faithful to the covenant, or the Covenant Maker.

End Results of Breaking the Covenant

- ✓ The calamity of the exile caused people to believe that God's promises had failed.
- ✓ People forgot that the covenant was conditional from a human perspective. Although God is always faithful to the covenant.
- ✓ The book of Daniel was written to re-establish faith in God and in His covenant promises, and to bring security and Hope to God's people.

More Details Emerge...

"This is what the LORD says: 'If you can break my covenant with the day and my covenant with the night, so that day and night no longer come at their appointed time (Jer. 33; 20)

.

Historical Background

In the book of Daniel we find five great themes that run parallel in EVERY CHAPTER. As we defined it earlier, a theme is the recurring teaching or point found in any document. These five great themes appear in every chapter, whether applicable to an individual or to a kingdom. Let's take a closer a look at this concept.

1. **Covenant:** A legal agreement between two parties.
2. **Wisdom:** The keeping or breaking of the covenant determines the wisdom of the vassal or his lack of it.
3. **Judgment:** God gives a probationary period to every person/kingdom involved with the covenant to test the loyalty of the parties involved in the covenant.
4. **Exaltation:** Every covenant keeper in the book of Daniel is exalted, while the covenant breaker is demoted or humiliated.
5. **Reward:** Whoever breaks the covenant gets the reward in terms of curses. The same is true for the covenant keepers, they get the reward in terms of blessings.

Facts to Be Considered About Daniel

- ✓ Some believe that Daniel was around 18 years old when he was brought to Babylon (White, 4T; p. 570).
- ✓ Daniel was most likely castrated based on the prophetic charts (2 Chron. 20; 18). We also find that he was among the "eunuchs."
- ✓ Daniel had lost his family, home and land and was given a new identity that began with the changing of his name to Belteshazzar (1;7).

- ✓ Daniel appeared to be the oldest one among the four young Hebrews (v.8).
- ✓ Daniel is never called “prophet” in the whole book.
- ✓ It was Jesus who called Daniel a prophet (Mat. 24:15)?
- ✓ Daniel became a wise man, a royal counselor and a royal Davidic figure (he was a prince from the kingdom of Judah)
- ✓ Daniel became the chief figure as a vassal of God in Babylon (Dan. 6;10).
- ✓ Daniel became the co-ruler with God of the Davidic dynasty, even in Babylon (Dan. 5;31).
- ✓ This in turn means that God was still faithful to His promises made to David as established in the covenant.

Questions to Be Answered

1. Identify the five themes in chapter one. Please name the verses in which those themes are found:
    a. Covenant________________________
    b. Wisdom__________________________
    c. Judgment________________________
    d. Exaltation_______________________
    e. Reward__________________________
2. If you were to lose everything as Daniel did, would you still believe that God cares about you?

3. Why do you think that Daniel never saw himself as a "prophet"?

4. In which way do you think that Daniel became the "Davidic" figure in the exile? Based on what fact?

5. If God decided to bless Daniel and his friends in Babylon, does that mean that He changed His mind and felt sorry for the people?

The Babylonian Welcome Party!

"But Daniel purposed in his heart that he would not defile himself with portions of the king's delicacies" (Dan. 1;8).

Historical Background

Nebuchadnezzar took the vessels from the temple in Jerusalem. It was a common belief that bringing the vessels from the temple of the conquered ones meant their God had also been conquered.

The king commanded Ashpenaz to bring into the palace certain of the "children" (BEN = descendant) among the conquered people (v. 3). They had to be young and tender, with no blemish, well favored, skillful in all wisdom, cunning in knowledge, understood in science (v. 4).

From among the Israelites, four young men were chosen: Daniel, Hananiah, Mishael and Azariah (v.6). The number 4 represents totality. These young men were representatives of the whole Hebrew nation. However, God allowed them to become "slaves" and "eunuchs" because of Israel's unfaithfulness to the covenant (2 Chron. 20:18).

The king himself appointed what they should eat (v.5). It is interesting that any training in life begins by looking into one's own diet. God's first commandment to man was about what he should eat and what not to eat (Gen. 2; 16).

The king also ordered a change of their Hebrew names to the Babylonian names: Belteshazzar, Shadrach, Mesach and Abed-nego (v.7).

Daniel's Choice

Daniel and his friends decided not to defile themselves with the food of the king (v.8). However, Daniel seems to eat meat in (10; 3). So, what's the problem?

- ✓ The food was dedicated first to the Babylonian gods and then served to the people.

- ✓ Therefore, the matter involved here is something more than eating; it is FAITHFULNESS TO THE COVENANT that is involved.

Therefore, Daniel requested legumes and produce such as: seeds and grains like, barley, wheat, rye, peas and nuts on a trial basis for 10 days (v.8) instead of the king's food that was rich in calories and alcohol based.

- ✓ Ten days (10) were given as a probationary time.
- ✓ The number 10 for the Babylonians meant the whole. It was used in the same sense as the number 7 among the Hebrews.

Questions to Be Answered

1. Who delivered the king of Judah into the hands of Nebuchadnezzar according to Dan. 1; 2?

2. Why do you think God would allow such a thing? Wasn't He supposed to "protect" His own people based on the covenant He made with them?

3. Why would God let His own chosen people to suffer into the hands of a king that was more pagan than His own people?

4. After the 10 days, how much wiser and stronger were the young Hebrews found to be in comparison to the others? (vv.15-20).

5. According to v.9, who gave Daniel and his friends "goodwill"?

6. Was Ashpenaz concern a valid one? (v.10).

7. What does the phrase of v. 21 mean to you in regards to WHEN and WHO wrote the book of Daniel?

A Forgotten Dream

"And the king said to them: I have had a dream and my spirit is anxious to know the dream" (Dan. 2;3).

Historical Background

Some studies on dreams suggest that dreams are just the residue of the thoughts of the brain. Allow me to explain:

- ✓ Everyday we are bombarded with thousands of stimuli through our senses. At sleep, our brain has the daunting task of filing every one of them.
- ✓ Usually, dreams happen just before waking up. If the brain did not have time to file all the stimuli, then it compresses all that information in one place to be sent to the "dump." This could explain why some of our dreams are so strange.
- ✓ Dreams can also be devastating or uplifting for many people even today.
- ✓ In religions like Voodoo, people believe that dreams can determine their fate.

The king had a dream and forgot about it. He decided to summon the wise men of Babylon to tell him what he had dreamed (Dan. 2; 3)

In ancient times, people believed that dreams were messages directly from the gods. Nebuchadnezzar was not oblivious to this reality (Job 33; 14-16).

In addition, the king's court was not very stable yet since he had been ruling for only 2 years. Apparently, not all the court appointments had been made by this time (Dan. 2; 1).

Therefore, the king offered to reward with gifts and honors whoever had WISDOM, and helps him to remember the dream (v.6). He was also ready to

CUT THEM IN PIECES if they failed to do what he was asking them to do (v.5).

The king promised three things if they were able to tell the forgotten dream: Gifts, Rewards and Honor. Almost every human being is looking for one or all of these three things.

The wise men were not able to answer such a request. The king issued a decree to kill all the wise men of Babylon.

The king was so outraged that he forgot that a nation couldn't survive without these wise people in it. Wise people are necessary for the proper function and survival of any entity whether is a family, a company, a church, a town or a nation.

Questions to Be Answered

1. Why was Nebuchadnezzar's spirit troubled? (v.1).

2. Apparently distress causes people to lose their sleep. How did Nebuchadnezzar deal with his insomnia? (v.2).

3. According to v.2 four different kinds of wise people were summoned: ________________, ________________, ____________,

__________________.

4. What sobering statement did the wise men make to the king in v. 10?

5. The wise men acknowledged the ultimate reality in v. 11. Can you name it?

God Is In Charge!

"Blessed be the name of God forever and ever... He removes kings and raises up kings..." (Dan. 2;20-21).

Historical Background

The king made the decision to kill every one of his counselors (Dan. 2; 12-13). They looked for Daniel and his friends to be executed (v.13).

However, the time that was denied to the rest of the wise men was granted to Daniel (v.16).

Daniel went back home and asked his friends to pray with him (v. 17).

This story encourages us to seek one another and to get together in prayer. When we pray, God can change our problems into golden opportunities.

A Thrilling Conversation

God revealed Nebuchadnezzar's dream to Daniel (v.19)

The king was intrigued to know if this young man will tell him the dream (v. 26). Daniel's answer was basically "NO, I CAN'T. But, there is a God in Heavens who is able (v.28)."

Daniel told the king that God is the true Ruler (Suzerain) of the earth. He revealed the king that true WISDOM is found only in the true God.

Daniel's speech of recognition should be repeated all the time:

- ✓ God changes times and seasons v.21).
- ✓ God sets and takes rulers away (v.21).
- ✓ It is God who gives WISDOM to the wise (v.21).
- ✓ It is God who REVEALS what is deep and hidden (v.22).
- ✓ Light dwells with God, and He knows what lays in darkness (v. 22).
- ✓ God is the One who gives the STRENGTH (v. 23).

- ✓ Wisdom and might are found in God alone (v.23).
- ✓ God is the One who makes secret things known to men (v.23).

Let's take a closer look at Nebuchadnezzar's dream.

Head of Gold = Babylon
(606 b. C - 539 b. C)

Chest of Silver = Medo-Persia
(539 b. C. - 331 b. C)

Belly/Thighs of Brass = Greece
(331 b. C - 168 b. C)

Legs of Iron = Rome
(168 b. C - 476 a. D)

Feet of Iron + Clay = Rome's
(476 a. D - until today) **division**

Questions to Be Answered

1. What four things did God give Nebuchadnezzar according to v.37? ____________, ____________, ______________, ____________.

2. All these kingdoms have come to pass as prophesied. What is the ultimate promise made by God in His dream? (v.44).

3. What is the meaning of the stone? (v.45). Compare with 1 Cor. 10; 4.

4. Why did God choose a dream instead of sending a prophet?

5. Isn't God arbitrarily allowing evil powers to rule?

The Real Issue

"...And the stone that struck the image became a great mountain and filled the whole earth" (Dan. 2;35).

Historical Background

Nebuchadnezzar thought that he was the sole ruler. God showed him that humans should rule under God's authority.

The Rock that came from heaven and pulverized the image became a great mountain/kingdom that filled the whole earth and lasted forever. This represents Christ's everlasting kingdom. Mountains were associated with the dwelling of the gods.

- ✓ Noah's ark ended its journey on mount Ararat (Gen. 8; 4).
- ✓ Abraham's sacrifice of Isaac was on mount Moriah (Gen. 22:2).
- ✓ When God appeared to Moses in the burning bush, He told him to bring the Israelites to Mount Sinai (Ex. 2; 12). He did indeed give them His laws (Ex. 19:2).
- ✓ It was on a mountain (Golgotha) where Jesus Christ was offered for the sins of the world (Mat. 27; 32-50).
- ✓ And the redeemed will stand on a mountain (Zion) at the end of all things (Rev. 14; 1).

Conclusion

God meets people at their level of understanding. But in every case, He lets people know that He is the sole Ruler. The issue here is rulership of the earth. Nebuchadnezzar thought he was ruling the earth; and he does (as God's co-regent) when he accepts the Rulership of the Most High God.

Questions to Be Answered

1. What does the image represent?

2. Who is the sole Ruler of the earth? (Psalms 22; 28)

3. Why does God allow kingdoms that do not follow Him to rule? (Read Exo. 7; 3-5 & Gen. 15; 16 to answer).

4. Isn't this a sign of weakness in God's style of leadership? (Ezeq. 18; 29-32).

5. What were mountains associated with? (Ezeq. 28; 15-16).

6. Why is God interested in meeting people's limited understanding of His purposes? (Isa. 1; 18)

7. At the end what did Nebuchadnezzar recognize about God's rulership? (Dan. 2; 47).

8. Number the five things that God gave to Nebuchadnezzar as a world ruler (vv. 37-38).
   a. ________________
   b. ________________
   c. ________________
   d. ________________
   e. ________________

After interpreting the dream, the king BOWED DOWN before Daniel and offered him "oblations" (mimchah - which is a bloodless sacrifice); and "sweet odors" (incense). When these two elements were presented to Daniel, they were a symbol of recognition as: (a) a king; (b) a semi-god; (c) or both.

- ✓ Please identify the five great themes (Covenant, Wisdom, Judgment, Exaltation and Reward) found in chapter 2.

A Modified Dream!

"And whoever does not fall down and worship, shall be cast immediately into the midst of a burning fiery furnace" (Dan. 2;6).

Historical Background

- ✓ Nebuchadnezzar quickly forgot who was the true Ruler of the world. He then decided to build a great image of pure gold (royal and divine metal). It was not the first time that he had made images to be worshipped. In fact, he made an image of himself (salam sarrutiya; Landong, XIX, B, col. x, 6).
- ✓ The dimensions of the image were 110ft high by 3ft wide. The event took place in "Dura" (duri-li), which means "God's rampart." The king ordered every one to bow down the newly made image. Daniel's friends decided to disobey the king's command.

There are decisions that should be made before hand. There are decisions that cannot wait until the last moment. It appears that this was the case of the three Hebrew young men. The king summoned eight types of officers:

Princes	=	Nobility
Governors	=	Dominion
Captains	=	Military
Judges	=	Judicial
Treasurers	=	Financial
Counselors	=	Sociological
Sheriffs	=	Protectors
Rulers	=	Legislative

These three men's disobedience did not ring well among some Chaldeans (Dan. 3;8, 12). They decided to speak against them before the king.

Everytime you decide to do the right thing before God, you will find others who will disagree and twist your motives.

The king acted correctly: (a) he investigated the matter in person. (b) he gave a warning. (c) he gave the three men a second chance.

These young men decided to defy the king's order following what Acts 5;18 says. We should never hesitate to do what is right in God's eyes.

The king had been very benevolent and reasonable with them. However, we should always stand for God, in spite of the favors we have received from human beings.

The king was left with no choice, but to give the order that these young men be cast into the fiery furnace.

Questions to Be Answered

1. What happened to the men that took up that three young Hebrews? (v.22).

2. What did Nebuchadnezzar see in the midst of the fiery furnace? (v.25)

3. With which title did Nebuchadnezzar address the young men according to v.26?

4. Can you summarize Nebuchadnezzar speech in one single sentence? (v. 28).

5. Do you think the king has learned his lesson about religious freedom and coercion? (v.29). Whatever is your answer explain why!

6. In terms of job related issues, what was the end result of these young men? (v.30).

Hidden Meaning Revealed!

"He reveals deep and secret things; He know what is in the darkness, and light dwells with Him" (Dan. 2;23).

Historical Background

- ✓ When God appears to human beings it is because He wants to communicate something very important. God's messages should be eagerly heard because He is the giver of the covenant. We have the responsibility to listen to what the king has to say.
- ✓ The Bible specifically mentions several elements in v. 27 that need further exploration. Let's take a closer look at them.

Hidden Meanings

Fire = Destructor Element (Gen. 19;24-25). Fire had no power on them. Fire could not destroy them at all.
Furnace = Afflictions (Deut. 4;20 / 1Kings 8;51). Quite often God saves people not from the afflictions, but through them.
Body = Life/Sacrifice (Ezek. 39;17-18). Their lives were in reality sacrificed to the Babylonian god-fire, but the Lord delivered them.
Hair = Dignity (Isa. 3;24 / Jer. 7;29). God protected the faithful covenant keepers from shame. Their dignity remained untouched.
Heads = Intelligence/Understanding (Eccles. 2;14 / Isa. 2;2). If you are faithful to the covenant, God might well preserve your intelligence and intellect from being destroyed by the enemy.
Servants of the Most High God = The three young Hebrews honored God with their lives. God honored them with power and worldwide recognition.

A Dangerous Decree

The king exceeded his limits and issued a decree forcing everyone to obey the only true God. However, God is not interested in worship that is mandatory. Worship and obedience that does not come from a grateful heart is exactly the kind of worship that God avoids.

The Real Issue

- ✓ Rulership over the conscience of people that transpires through worship.
- ✓ The king exceeded his limits in forcing people to accept one particular belief system.

Questions to Be Answered

1. In how many ways does God speak to people according to Heb 1;1-3?

2. Why do you think God spoke to a "pagan" king through a revelation of Himself in the fiery furnace?

3. How can we know when the vision is from God according to Num 24;3-4?

4. Please identify the five (5) great themes that run parallel in every chapter in Daniel: Covenant, Wisdom, Judgment, and Exaltation, Reward.

5. Why must the desire to serve God come from the heart?

6. What is the danger of trying to **force** others to believe like we do?

7. Is there a danger in trying to **impose** our beliefs system on others?

Mad By Decree!

"...The Most High rules in the kingdom of men, gives it to whomever He will" (Dan. 4;17).

Historical Background

- ✓ 13 people out of 100 commit suicide due to a mental illness.
- ✓ 1 in 10 people of ages 12 and over, take anti-depressant medication regularly.
- ✓ 15% of those have been using anti-depressant for over 10 years.
- ✓ 40% of females as opposed to 20% males are more prone to take this kind of medication at any given time.
- ✓ White caucasians lead this trend with four (4) times higher numbers of taking medications than any other race.

Another Dream For The King

In this case, the king did not forget the dream. However, he could not understand what it meant. Once again, Daniel was brought in to interpret the dream.

Details of The Dream

1. A big tree that sustained the life of every creature on earth (Dan. 4;11-12).
2. The tree was cut off and the fruits and branches spreaded and the animals chased out (v.14).
3. The stump and roots were left in the earth bound with a band of iron (v.15).
4. The heart of the tree (man) was changed into the heart of a beast (v.16).
5. This whole ordeal was by decision of the "Watchers" (v.17).
6. This was done to teach a lesson to those who rule: God is in charge! (v.17).

Interesting Facts

- ✓ The king recognized that Daniel was filled with the Holy Spirit of God (v.18).
- ✓ Daniel seemed to be afraid of revealing to the king the meaning of the dream (v.19).
- ✓ Nebucchadnezzar recognized that God declares: signs, wonders; and that God's kingdom is everlasting (vv.2-3).

Questions to Be Answered

1. What was the primary reason for this decree against Nebuchadnezzar according to Dan. 4;27?

2. What co-relation do you see between Daniel's counsel and God's counsel to the leaders of His people? (Lev. 25;17).

3. Why do you think God commanded to let the land rest in the 7th year? (Lev. 25;3-4).

4. Do you see any relationship between the seven years of God's people being free from oppression from the king and the Jubilee (Lev. 25;13-17)?

5. Please identify the five main themes found in every chapter in the book of Daniel: Covenant, Wisdom, Judgment, and Exaltation, Reward.

What Have You Done?

"This decree is by the decision of the holy Watchers, and the sentence by the word of the holy Ones" (Dan. 4;17).

Historical Background

1. The "Holy Watchers" are in reality the Supreme Court Members of heaven. This body of beings has the authority and power to make determinations on behalf or against human beings.
2. This grand Jury has various names in the Bible:
   a. The Council of El (God) (Job 15;8).
   b. Council of Eloah (PSalm 82;1).
   c. Council of Yahweh (Jer. 23;18).
   d. Council of the Holy Ones (Psalms 89;5,7).
3. In ancient times, the courtiers discussed the issues among themselves (1 Kings 22) and the king (the presiding judge) listened carefully.
4. When all the members of the Grand Jury agree on a decision, then the king or presiding judge dictates the sentence.
5. This Grand Jury decides the following issues:
   a. Life/death/fate.
   b. Inheritance.
   c. Rulership

Judgment to The King

- In the case of King Nebuchadnezzar, he was found guilty of "oppression" (v.27); "iniquity" (v.27); "sin" (v.27) and "pride" (v.30).
- In this case, the wise men were summoned again to interpret the king's dream. Once again, of Daniel it is said: "the spirit of the Holy God is in you" (v.9).
- At the "end of twelve months" (v.29), judgment is passed upon the king. This period (12 months) was a probationary time given to the king to see if he would repent according to Daniel's counsel (v.27).

- The sentence was given and Nebuchadnezzar became mad for seven years (v.25).
- The king's mental illness is known today as "Boanthropy" (a delusional state of mind where the person believes he is something or someone else).

Judgment Issues

1. No human being is sentenced without being given a probationary time to repent.
2. God alone does not make the decisions for the judgment; decisions are made by the Grand Jury presided by God Himself.
3. The sentence given to every human will always fit the crime. In the case of King Nebuchadnezzar, his pride was the issue; therefore, he needed to be humiliated.
4. For seven years, Nebuchadnezzar lost his mind. He became insane and wild. Conclusion? Sin disfigures the image of God in him.

Implications

- It is after the king recognized that the Most High ruled, when his mind was restored (v.34).
- A return to the covenant brings the blessings instead of the curses (v.36).
- The king recognized that no one could tell God "What have you done?" (v.35).

Questions to Be Answered

1. In your opinion, what is the main cause of so many mentally ill people these days?

2. Why do you think judgment is important?

3. Please find the five great themes in chapter 4 (Covenant, Wisdom, Exaltation, Judgment, Reward).

The Last Party!

"In the same hour the fingers of a man's hand appeared... And the king saw the part of the hand that wrote" (Dan. 5;5).

Historical Background

1. Cyrus and Darius (Medo-Persians) were at war with Belshazzar the new king of Babylon.
2. Belshazzar (grandson of Nebuchadnezzar) is the ruling king of Babylon (Dan. 5;1).
3. He offered a feast to 1000 of his officials (v.1).
4. The party became a drunken orgy (v.2).
5. Totally drunk, the king ordered to use the cups that had been dedicated for sacred use in the temple of God in Jerusalem. His grandfather transported them when he conquered Jerusalem (Dan. 1;1-2).
6. Now everyone when and defiled what was sacred (Dan. 5;3).

Questions to Be Answered

1. According to v.4, how many items are mentioned that the king and his people worshipped?

2. Who judged Belshazzar according to vv 17, 24?

3. Verses 17 and 24 seem to contradict each other. How would you explain it?

4. What was written on the wall? (v.25).

5. In terms of judgment, what the writing on the wall meant?

6. Why was the king terrified? (vv 5-6)

7. What three things did Belshazzar offer to whomever would read the writing on the wall and interpret it? (v.7).

8. Who came in to counsel the king? (v.10).

9. Please write down the three most important things (for you) that the queen said about Daniel (vv.11-12).

Reflections

1. The king's lack of wisdom cost him his life and his kingdom (vv.30-31).
2. Daniel improvised a speech for the king and his courtiers (vv17-24) Look at the most important points of it:
    - Men's rewards/gifts mean nothing if they are not endorsed by God (v.17).
    - God was the one who gave him the kingdom (v.18).
    - People were conquered by God's intervention (v.19).
    - God taught Nebuchadnezzar a painful lesson on humility (v.20).
    - God APPOINTS as a ruler to whomever He wants (v.21).
    - Belshazzar saw God's hand working in his kingdom (v.22).
    - The king led his people to drunkenness and sexual orgies (v.23)
    - The king and his people praised false gods (v.23).
    - God had given Belshazzar his whole life to repent and he never did (v.22). Therefore, he ran out of time (v.24).

3. Please identify the five great themes (Covenant, Wisdom, Exaltation (or lack of it), Judgment, Reward).

Deciphering The Writing!

"There is a man in your kingdom in whom is the Spirit of the Holy God" (Dan. 5;11).

Historical Background

- The king and his officers were so drunk (prov. 31;3-5) and confused (Prov.23;19-21/, that they could not even read what was written on the wall (Dan. 5;7).

The Writing Itself

1. Mene = God counted your kingdom.
2. Tekel = God weighed your kingdom and you were found wanting.
3. Peres = God divided your kingdom and it is given to the Medes and Persians.

Questions to Be Answered

1. If those cups taken from God's temple had not been used for many years, why did God take offense?

2. The Bible says that God "*delivered*" those temple vessels into the hands of the Babylonian kingdom, why did God seem upset about it now?

3. Why is so important to God not to defile what He has made holy? What is that telling you about the Sabbath according to Isaiah 56;2?

Judgment On Belshazzar

- ✓ When Daniel is called in, he seems not to have respect for king Belshazzar at all (Dan. 5;17). Daniel never said: "O king, live for ever," which was a common thing to say by any courtier when introduced to speak to the king.

- ✓ There are three main verbs in Daniel's explanation of the writing on the wall:
  - Counted
  - Weighed
  - Divided

1. The Bible says that God even has our hair "*numbered*" (Mat. 10;30).
2. At some point, Job even asked God to "*weigh*" him in "*honest scales*" (Job 31;10).
   - ✓ Therefore, it is important to God to judge individuals and those in positions of power as well as kingdoms!
   - ✓ Daniel was able to be the instrument used by God to save Nebuchadnezzar, but he could not do much with his grandson Belshazzar. This means that we are not always successful in soul winning, but this should not discourage us.

Questions to Be Answered

1. Is God "counting" every deed we make? If so, on the basis of what can He save us?

2. Doesn't this "counting" contradict the Scriptures elsewhere where it says that we are saved by grace alone and not by works of our own?

3. How can we reconcile the idea that we are **saved by grace**, but at the same time we are **judged by works**? Please use the Bible alone to answer this question.

4. Please identify the five great themes found in every chapter in the book of Daniel (Covenant, Wisdom, Exaltation, Judgment, Reward).

Without Fault! Hummmm...?

"*We shall not find any charge against this Daniel unless we find it against him concerning the law of his God" (Dan. 5;5).*

Historical Background

1. Darius became the co-ruler with Cyrus. They diverted the river, entered into Babylon and killed Belshazzar. The Bible specifically says "Darius the Mede received the kingdom" (Dan. 5;31). This very well could mean that he received the kingdom from Daniel.
2. Darius divided the kingdom in 120 provinces and placed three governors (40 provinces each -Dan. 6;1).
3. Daniel was one of the three main governors (v.1).
4. We also read that Daniel was "*superior*" to the rest of the governors (v.3).
5. Daniel "*distinguished himself*" concerning his job or his character (v.3).
6. The reason for this distinction was because an "excellent spirit was in him" (v.3).
7. The king (Darius) sought to set Daniel up "*above the other governors.*" Therefore, they hated Daniel and plotted to get rid of him (v.4).

Spiritual Applications

- ✓ God wants to find men and women that can be faithful, without faults, especially at the work place and at home.
- ✓ When the Spirit of God is in you, everyone will notice that you have an excellent spirit.
- ✓ When you are right with God, Satan will try to use your own faithfulness against you.

The Plot

1. Daniel's enemies plotted to kill him, but nothing was found against Daniel, because he was faithful (v.4).
2. The only thing that his enemies realized they could use against him was his own faithfulness (v.5).
3. The other governors devised a plan and lied to Darius about it (v.7).
4. These evil men flattered the vanity of the new king under the disguise of praying to him alone for 30 days (v.7).
5. The king did not see that one coming.
   a. Envy can blind people to the point of wishing the death of a faithful person.

Questions to Be Answered

1. Why do you think these men lied to the king? (v.7).

2. Read Dan. 6;10 and answer, why is Daniel praying openly and publicly?

3. Is not this a contradiction of Jesus' own counsel on how to pray? (Mat. 6;6).

4. Why is this public prayer important to Daniel and for God's people in terms of the Davidic covenant? Please re-read the lesson: "More Details Emerge..." to answer this question.

5. Why did Daniel's windows have to be opened "*towards Jerusalem*"? (v.10 -Please read 1 Kings 8;48-50).

Delivered From! Not Of...

"He delivers and rescues, and He works signs and wonders..." (Dan. 6;27).

Historical Background

- ✓ Evil co-workers plotted against Daniel and succeeded in luring the king to force religion on people (Dan. 6;6-8).
- ✓ Daniel continued praying like he would normally do it, even AFTER knowing of the decree (v.10).
- ✓ The plotters went together to hear Daniel pray to his God (v.11).
- ✓ They rushed into Darius' courtroom to tell him the news about Daniel (v.12).
- ✓ Darius wasn't happy about the news and realized that he had been tricked and tried by all means to deliver Daniel from the sentence to die by lions (v.14).
- ✓ King Darius made a confession that needs to resonate among all of us. Please read it in verse 16.

Questions to Be Answered

1. How did Darius know that Daniel served God "continually"? (v.16).

2. Why do you think that Darius believed that the God of Daniel could deliver him from the lions? (v.16).

3. Darius thought that a decree to pray to him would establish him in the kingdom. In your opinion, why was he wrong?

4. The three young Hebrews defied Nebuchadnezzar and it was, in a way, easy for them because they could encourage one another. However, Daniel is alone in this entire ordeal. How

can we deal with problems ALONE when there is no one to encourage us?

5. What did the king do early in the morning the day after Daniel was cast into the lion's den? (v.19).

6. What was Darius' hope about Daniel and his God? (v.20).

7. Please read Darius' decree and write down the main points of that speech (vv.25-27).

8. Please find the five great themes of the book of Daniel (Covenant, Wisdom, Exaltation, Judgment, Reward).

Final Thoughts

- ✓ It would be a powerful testimony if people could see that we serve God "continually" (vv.16, 20)
- ✓ It would be more powerful if people could see that we serve a God that saves (vv.16, 20).
- ✓ In the human trial, Daniel was found guilty and sentenced to death. But in God's courtroom, Daniel was found INNOCENT (v.22); therefore, he was delivered from death.
- ✓ The accusers were thrown into the lion's den and devoured immediately; even their bones were broken/eaten (v.24).
- ✓ Daniel was in exile. But he was faithful and served God continually. We all live exiled from the glory of God, but can we be faithful even in these circumstances?
- ✓ I hope you and I can be faithful to God and may we serve Him CONTINUALLY! God bless you all...

www.ingramcontent.com/pod-product-compliance
Ingram Content Group UK Ltd.
Pitfield, Milton Keynes, MK11 3LW, UK
UKHW041902190726
13854UKWH00003B/1052